DANIEL McADAMS

BIBLICAL
EXPLANATIONS:
The Paranormal

Trilogy Christian Publishers

A Wholly Owned Subsidiary of Trinity Broadcasting Network
2442 Michelle Drive
Tustin, CA 92780

Manufactured in the United States of America
10 9 8 7 6 5 4 3 2 1
Library of Congress Cataloging-in-Publication Data is available.
ISBN: 978-1-63769-002-4
E-ISBN: 978-1-63769-003-1

FORWARD

"What if ghosts are actually demons?" That's the question that
I saw when I looked at my phone a while ago. I texted back "Sure, it
could be a possibility." In my mind, though, the response was more
like, "Yeah, right, I've heard that before and I don't buy it. Sorry, but
no." I was glad to see that Daniel was delving deeper into theology
and the Scriptures, and it was causing me to spend more time on my
Christianity as well, but I basically almost laughed off the question
with a tone of, "Well, that's just the more legalistic, older folks in the
church who want to write off the paranormal things we have going
on here on Earth. I thought we'd written that one off some time ago,
but I suppose we haven't after all."

This piece is definitely something that's going to be hard to
swallow for many people. It's a blow to the pride, especially to
people like Daniel and I who have spent years out there in the field

looking for "the truth." I wrestled with it for a while as a pride issue, and also my own human mind thinking that I could figure it out; and that I knew what I was doing. They're ghosts, spirits of dead human beings, not demons. I've spent nearly a decade with that belief and experiencing things that point towards that fact with my own eyes and ears. I've got it all figured out.

As hard to believe as it is, I didn't have it all figured out. And, equally novel of a concept, the only place I needed to look to find the truth was sitting on my bookshelf (admittedly gathering some dust): The Bible. Thankfully, our God is a gracious and loving God because He started moving me into thought on the question. I began to realize, still somewhat to my disappointment, that it did answer a lot of questions we had about the paranormal.

The more I thought about it, the more I realized that it had to be the answer. The more that Daniel and I started to discuss and explore the Bible, the more I saw how wrong I was. Not only on a factual basis, but even more disturbingly, on a theological basis. Like too many people out there, I was guilty of making the Word fit my own beliefs than making my own beliefs fit the Bible. A quick look at a few fundamental questions of paranormal investigation shows this:

- How are souls of the formerly living still here on Earth, not in Heaven or Hell? Well obviously, they're waiting for Jesus to return; we'll be risen back up then our souls will go to where they're supposed to. Wrong!
- Why, then, do only certain people become ghosts? And why is it that we can only talk to ghosts dating back maybe two or three hundred years at the most? Shouldn't there be literally billions of ghosts out there, including people from the very beginning of human history? Well, that's a good question that I'll figure out eventually. (Hint: There's also a very clear answer for this that I was ignoring)
- How do ghosts operate? What does the other side look like and how do ghosts do what they do? In all of my experience, and

as far as I knew, no investigators had ever had any question on the mechanics of the afterlife answered for them. With all those billions of former humans roaming around, you'd think that somebody would be nice enough to explain a little bit (or, you know, the ghosts of some paranormal investigators that would just love to answer the questions they used to ask). Now that I look back on it, it's clear to me now. Because a demon isn't going to answer questions like that!

I grew up in the church all my life. I was formally saved in July of 2002. I definitely considered myself a Christian and if asked at the time, I would have even told you that I was a strong Christian. I would now have to say that I really wasn't that strong of a Christian at all. And thankfully, I've been blessed with enough courage and humility to be able to admit that. The great thing about our God, however, is that He gives us an endless set of chances to change what's in our hearts and in our minds.

I'm still reluctant in some ways to follow the path that He's shown me through study of the Word relating to the paranormal. I'm constantly reminded of Matthew 16:24, *"Then Jesus said to his disciples, 'If any of you wants to be my follower, you must give up your own way, take up your cross, and follow me.'"* (NLT)

The fact of the matter is this is the way things are. Whether we like it or not, there's no arguing with the Word of God. Whether we like it or not, the conclusions reached in what you're about to read are true; not because Daniel and I are experts in the paranormal, experts on theology, or because we're infallible, or anything else to do with us but because the conclusions are based directly upon the words of, He who IS infallible.

I've had to humble myself before the Lord many times to even attach my name to this project. My pride and human mind don't want to allow me to publicly say what Daniel and I are saying. I've spent so many years of my life investigating the paranormal and building my credibility as a paranormal investigator. I've spent so much time and effort putting myself out there in this community and striving to become a recognizable name in the field of paranormal investigation. Being attached to this project is almost certainly going to throw away all that time and it is going to erase my credibility. I'm probably going to even lose friends I've made along the way, or at least change our friendships. Beyond a shadow of a doubt this is going to ensure that I'm not going to be taken with any seriousness by 99.9% of paranormal investigators. And that is something that is a hard blow to my human ego and the selfish parts of my heart. So, in closing, I'm going to leave a few passages that have spoken to me in the hopes that you can use their wisdom to help you on your own journey throughout this text and if you choose to accept what's put forward here, hopefully these verses will help quiet your mind and center you in the commands of our Father rather than the desires of our flesh.

I have given them Your word; and the world has hated them because they are not of the world, just as I am not of the world. I do not pray that You should take them out of the world, but that You should keep them from the evil one. They are not of the world, just as I am not of the world. Sanctify them by Your truth. Your word is truth. John 17:14-17 (NKJV)

Therefore, brothers and sisters, in view of the mercies of God, I urge you to present your bodies as a living sacrifice, holy and pleasing to God; this is your true worship. Do not be conformed to this age, but be transformed by the renewing of your mind, so that you may discern what is the good, pleasing, and perfect will of God. Romans 12:1-2 (CSB)

God bless in all you do,
Dillon Dick

Aubrey, Texas 19 September 2019

INTRODUCTION

"Dillon, I just heard a growl in the boiler room behind me. We need to go figure out what is back there and making these sounds." I said as we were investigating strange, paranormal occurrences that were happening on the upper level of an old theater during a paranormal conference we were attending.

"Alright." he replied.

We grabbed our cameras and made our way into the boiler room, unsure of what we would find. As we walked further in, I noticed an old dentist chair just sitting on the floor.

"I am going to sit in this old dentist chair and see if that doesn't elicit a response." I said.

As I walked up to the chair and got ready to sit down, I suddenly heard a loud bang on the wall.

"Did you hear that?" I asked. "There was just a loud bang on the wall next to me."

Suddenly, without warning, I began feeling incredibly anxious and my skin felt clammy. My brain had stopped processing both sight and sound and I knew something was wrong. Very wrong. I was no longer in full control of my body. Something was trying to take control of me, and my body was reacting. I immediately knew that I was being oppressed and that something was trying to possess me. I opened my mouth to inform Dillon of what was going on, but nothing came out. Panic started to set in now. I opened my mouth to try to tell Dillon I was being either oppressed or possessed, but again, no words left my mouth. I opened my mouth a third time and all I could say was, "I can't talk." I noticed that my camera was pointed at the floor and as any good videographer would do, adjusted my camera so that it was pointing up. Then my brain again stopped processing the signals my eyes were sending it. I had no clue where Dillon was and, if he was saying anything, I couldn't hear it. At some point, two other investigators from the event entered the room. I knew they were talking to us, but I could hear no words. The only time I could hear anything was when one of them mentioned, "Oh wow. It just hit 66.6 degrees." Odd and unnerving that I was only able to process hearing that but nothing else. My mind was in a fog and I was doing my best to fight off whatever was trying to take me over. I would not give up.

"What's going on, Daniel?" one of the other investigators asked. Somehow, I was able to hear this question.

I turned toward him, and a huge, sarcastic smile split my face from ear to ear as I replied, "I can't talk." That was, but wasn't, me replying. Whatever energy, or thing, was trying to possess me was replying to him and laughing about what was going on. My brain was still not processing vision and was only processing whatever this thing would allow me to hear. Then, without notice, I said, "Okay. We need to get out of here. We need to leave this room. Whoa! Whatever had ahold of me just left me. Wow. Okay. Yeah, I'm back but I need to leave this room." And just like that, I was back to being me.

What felt like an eternity of fighting off this entity turned out to be only two minutes long. I left the boiler room and went downstairs, and a couple other investigators saw me and stated that I looked deathly pale and asked if I was alright. I said I was fine but Dillon and the others came down and also commented about my pale looks and told me I needed to step outside and get out of the building. So, I did. For over two years I was too afraid to go back and watch the footage from that night. I knew something was trying to possess and take over me and it was unsettling to think about watching it. Finally, after two years, I worked up my courage and watched the video from both my camera and Dillon's camera. I looked lost and detached from everything that was going on around me. My face was hollow and emotionless. That is until I replied to the other investigator's question and my skin crawled when I saw my smile and heard my response. But nothing could prepare me for what we captured on camera shortly after the attempted possession started. My camera captured a faint voice saying, "It's what you crave." And either me replying with a "Yeah" or the entity saying "Dan." My blood chilled when I watched Dillon's camera of this moment. I was staring blankly ahead, and my lips and mouth start slightly moving when these words are heard. It was talking to me using my own voice.

This is the first time I have gone public with this encounter that I had back in 2016. Up until this encounter, I had been investigating the paranormal for a little over five years. I had considered myself to be a good Christian, an expert on the paranormal, and thought I was prepared for anything. Boy was I wrong. This experience opened my eyes to what was out there and showed me that I had no idea what I was dealing with. After reviewing the footage two years later and seeing for myself what happened, I suddenly had a major desire to reevaluate my Christian faith. My immediate response following what happened was to pursue a secular, paranormal based education, and certifications to try to figure out and understand the paranormal better and build my credibility in the field. I worked hard to build my credibility and my expertise in the field, as well as that of my team. That is how I spent the two years between the actual experience and reviewing the video footage. Then, in 2019, I returned to my home church at the time, Chapel in The Hills, and met Pastor Todd Fletcher. The way he preached opened my eyes as his teaching of Scripture and biblical truths hit home and made me realize I was nowhere near where I needed to be in my walk with God or in my understanding of His Word. Of all the education I pursued, and research I conducted to try to seek out answers and understand the paranormal, I had not once actually turned to the Creator of the universe and His Word. This realization pushed me to pursue a path of theological and biblical studies to grow my faith, grow closer in my walk with the Lord and to understand the spiritual side of His creation from a Godly, biblical perspective and to be able to help people who had gone through, or are currently going through, an experience similar to mine, whether to a lesser, similar or greater degree.

Over the last couple years, my studies of the Scripture have led me to realize that the Bible holds many answers to paranormal questions and theories that are out there. I couldn't believe that I had spent almost a decade of my life pursuing answers to paranormal phenomena when so many of the answers were sitting in my Bible on my shelf, just waiting for me to open it up and embrace it. These studies have since led me to writing this book. Through my personal studies and research, through discussions with Dillon, my best friend and former fellow paranormal investigator who is also pursuing biblical and theological studies, and through some experiences and things I noticed at a paranormal conference we were invited to speak at, I realized I needed to sit down and get these biblical answers out there. I know this is not going to sit well with many paranormal investigators, both the religious and non-religious ones. I know this is going to be a slap in the face to all the psychics and mediums out there too. And I am well aware that if you are not a Christian yourself, you will more likely than not blow this book off and dismiss me and everything I say. But I urge you, as many of you tell skeptics and debunkers yourselves, please keep an open mind as you read this and consider the points I am making.

It has taken a lot of wrestling with pride and my own self to go through with writing this book. As Dillon said in the forward, he and I both worked our tails off to establish our names and the name of our team in the field of paranormal research as experts and professionals. With publishing this book with my name on it, I know that I am going to be blacklisted and shunned by many in the paranormal community, and that the near decade of work I put into building my credibility will be all for naught. But that is okay. Why? First and foremost, the world needs to know that they are dealing with demons and be exposed to the biblical truths about what the paranormal world really is. Hollywood and mainstream media have embraced the paranormal and spiritual world and enjoy flooding us with movies and shows about the dark and demonic.

As a follower of Christ, I cannot, and will not, just sit back and not tell people about the truth that is found in the Bible. Secondly, many of you who know me in the paranormal field will know that I have always said that I am not married to the idea of proving that the paranormal is real or not, but that I am married to finding and discovering the truth, whatever that may be. I have said that during many talks I have given about the paranormal. And I have found the truth. Thus, even if I lose everything in the field of paranormal research, this is a win-win for me. Why can I say that? The first win is because this has brought me closer in my walk with God, strengthened my faith and led me into a deeper understanding of Scripture. The second win is because I now have a fuller understanding of what the paranormal world is and have answers to many of the questions and theories that I had concerning the world of ghost hunting.

It's funny how a simple conversation about the paranormal at the beginning of 2019 with my boss at the time, led to the writing of this book. I realized that for the majority of the questions he asked, my response was along the lines of, "Well, I can't explain it. But that is why I go out into the field. Looking for answers." Wow, and I considered myself an expert in the field and I couldn't give him even one solid answer?

"Well, what are ghosts and spirits?" he asked.

I espoused the common theories and ideas about what ghosts and spirits are, when suddenly a thought I had not considered for a very long time popped into my head from out of the blue and I blurted out, "And there is a possibility that they are all actually demons." I am shocked at how true that statement actually turned out to be.

Thank you and God bless.
Daniel McAdams

TABLE OF CONTENTS

Chapter 1
WHO I AM

Before we go any further, let me introduce myself. You probably have the notion that I am some goody two shoes, holier than thou Bible thumping person who has never really believed in the paranormal in their life. Someone who only believes what religion or church has taught me. Let me stop you there. My first paranormal experience happened when I was seven or eight years old. Fast forward ten years and I was watching a television show about America's Eight Most Haunted. I hadn't planned on watching that TV show, but the show I was watching beforehand ended, and as TV stations like to do, America's Eight Most Haunted started playing immediately, and before I could grab the remote. I saw a building that I was familiar with in the show intro, so I sat back to see why that building was considered one of America's most haunted. I was hooked. I wanted to experience what I heard in people's stories and eyewitness accounts for myself. I started reading up on and researching the paranormal, and a year later, my best friend Dillon and I discovered that we had a mutual interest in the paranormal and we decided to start our own paranormal investigation team.

Over the course of almost a decade, we were very active in paranormal investigation. We would go out and investigate, hoping to have our own experiences and document evidence and gather data to research these phenomena. We spoke at paranormal conferences and on podcasts. Whilst we both are Christians, we pursued answers to many of the prevalent theories of paranormal investigation. We believe there is a Heaven and Hell, so instead of looking for "life after death" proof, we were more interested in finding out why the spirits of the dead seemed to hang around?

How do EVPs work? How are psychics able to communicate with spirits and discover the information they reveal? How are spirits able to talk to us, interact with us and manifest themselves visually for us? Are pets/animals able to see spirits? Among other questions. We committed ourselves to objective research and investigation and focused on making sure we were credible and open minded about all the research and investigation we did. I was so committed to this field, that I even pursued online education in parapsychology, as well as certification as a paranormal investigator, to further my knowledge and credibility in the field. And then in 2019, I decided to pursue theological studies and started going to church again. And when I examined the paranormal from a biblical and theological perspective, I was blown away.

I was shocked to see just how much the Bible has to say concerning the spiritual world and why it is not something to get involved in, beyond just the, "God says it is wrong" answer I had received over and over again when I first started. It saddened me to realize that so many pastors, church leaders, and Christians here in America are so ill equipped and lacking in knowledge concerning what the paranormal world actually is, as well as how to deal with it. Too many Christian and church leaders are quick to blow off any claims about the paranormal as being "just your imagination" or a silly idea. Too many Christians and church leaders don't know how to sit down and talk to someone about the paranormal and the spiritual world beyond the normal "God says it is wrong so don't get involved." These realizations were a driving force behind why I wrote this book. This book isn't to glorify my stories and experiences, nor is it meant to be a spotlight on me and what I was involved in and was saved from. This book is meant to be a resource for non-believers, regular Christians, and church leaders alike. This book is solely written to the glory of God and to explain from a biblical perspective the truth behind what the paranormal world really is. I am not here to tell you that none of this is real, because it all is very much real. Just not how you think.

Chapter 2
DO GHOSTS AND SPIRITS EXIST?
WHAT ARE THEY?

Let's get started by tackling two of the biggest questions in the field of paranormal investigation. Do ghosts and spirits exist/is there an invisible, spirit world? And if so, what are they? Let's answer that first question first, then the second question after we answer the first question.

The answer to the first question is: yes. There is a spiritual realm that is very much real. That means that spirit beings are real. There is an invisible world that is just as real as the visible world. If the spiritual world of angels and demons is not reality, neither is the Bible. *"For our struggle is not against flesh and blood, but against the rulers, against the authorities, against the powers of this dark world and against the spiritual forces of evil in the heavenly realms."* (Ephesians 6:12 NIV). The heavenly realms in this passage refers to the spiritual world. Flesh and blood are the visible world. If you look in the Old Testament, we see in 2 Kings 6:8-23 an example of the invisible world being revealed to a human. The king of Aram was trying to kill the prophet Elisha and had tracked him down. He had the city Elisha was staying in surrounded. Elisha's servants were afraid for their lives, fearing that they would be captured at any moment. But Elisha was calm and unafraid, and he prayed that his servant's eyes might be open to see the reality of God's army. *"So, he (Elisha) answered, 'Do not fear, for those who are with us are more than those who are with them.'"* (2 Kings 6:16 NKJV). For a moment, the invisible realm became visible and the servant was in awe as he saw God's heavenly forces ready to fight a supernatural battle for His servants. *"And Elisha prayed, and said, 'Lord, I pray,*

3

open his eyes that he may see.' Then the Lord opened the eyes of the young man, and he saw. And behold, the mountain was full of horses and chariots of fire all around Elisha." (2 Kings 6:17 NKJV). The rationalism of the Greco-Roman culture at the time of the New Testament, people who had grown intellectually sophisticated through complicated Greek philosophy and who had grown up in the Roman-era political and social modernization, also believed in the reality of an invisible realm and invisible spirits.

But what does the Bible say about demons? Does it affirm their existence as well? It sure does! When you read in the New Testament, you will often see Jesus and the apostles confronting Satan and demons. In fact, many of the miracles Jesus performed were in direct response to demonic activity and lies. Jesus Himself had many personal interactions with Satan and demons. The demons also always recognized Jesus as the Son of God. They knew who He was, and He knew who they were. Jesus would also not hesitate to accuse false teachers of being under satanic influence. We must keep in mind that all the writers of the New Testament were not making up any stories. They were writing either firsthand experiences or from eyewitnesses. This very clearly shows us that there is a very real and present invisible world that has influence over our visible world today as it did then.

What does this mean exactly? It means that if you deny the existence of Satan or demons or a spiritual world, you are rejecting the Word of God and Jesus Himself. You are then saying that the Bible made a mistake and is therefore not trustworthy. To impose our own viewpoint or beliefs on what the Bible says is to be claiming, whether we intend to or not, that we know better than God. Sadly, many Christians today try to impose a naturalistic worldview on the Bible, and in doing so, are granting small victories to Satan and his demons.

There is very much a real invisible world. The spiritual world is alive and active and full of entities. But what are these entities?

These entities consist of angels, demons and even Satan himself. Now that we have answered the first question, let's answer the second one, "What are they?" I am going to venture to say that 99.9% of interactions that paranormal investigators and ghost hunters have with spirits are encounters and interactions with demons. This includes intelligent and residual hauntings, poltergeists, and everything else. Why do I say that basically all spirits encountered on ghost hunts are demons and not angels? Because angels are supernatural beings created to do God's will. They are His messengers and are sent at His command. There is no biblical evidence that would support a claim that angels can decide on their own volition when, where and how they are going to show up to humankind. And I am pretty certain that knocking on walls, throwing things around, opening and closing doors, making footsteps, speaking through EVP or spirit boxes and all the other paranormal phenomena we encounter are not on God's "to-do list" for His will. *"Praise the Lord, you his angels, you mighty ones who do His bidding, who obey His word."* (Psalms 103:20 NIV). An angel is not going to try to make us think that there is life after death or ways to talk to our deceased friends and loved ones or discern historical facts or details about a location or particular spirit, as those are all contrary to God's will. Demons on the other hand, their entire goal is to get people to turn from God and to destroy humans as we are created in God's image. *"So, God created mankind in his own image, in the image of God he created them; male and female he created them."* (Genesis 1:27 NIV). Satan and his demons want to destroy those who believe in God and blind those who don't. If this means causing a believer to stumble and question God and truth by looking into the occult and believing in ghosts and spirits, then perfect. If this means causing a non-believer to be blind to God and truth by making them believe or look for life after death through interactions with spirits and ghosts, then perfect, mission accomplished.

Even though there are many non-believers and many scientists and educated persons who are quick to dismiss any notion of the paranormal being real, we need to remember that the idea of disembodied spirits and ghosts wandering around is not a new thing. All throughout history there are recordings of occult manifestations and paranormal happenings. In the Old Testament, the Bible often talks about Israel adopting and undertaking occult practices, rituals, and beliefs as they strayed from God. Cultural groups and peoples across the world and across the ages of history have all reported very similar stories and sightings of ghosts and strange happenings. And when a person has an extraordinary experience with a paranormal phenomenon, it can have powerful consequences and change a person's worldview and idea of what is actually real. And sadly, in today's age, even though the idea and belief in ghosts is not new, the paranormal and spiritual world is portrayed by the media as fun, harmless, and exciting.

Wow. There you have it. We have answered two of the biggest questions in the field of paranormal research. Are ghosts and spirits real/is there a spirit world? And if so, what are they? Let's move on and take a look now at what the Bible says about death and life after death.

Chapter 3
DEATH AND LIFE AFTER DEATH

"The dead know not anything, neither have they any more a reward; for the memory of them is forgotten. Also, their love, and their hatred, and their envy, is now perished; neither have they any more a portion forever in anything that is done under the sun... For there is no work, nor device, nor knowledge, nor wisdom, in the grave."

Ecclesiastes 9:5-6, 10 (NKJV)

For many paranormal investigators, their main mission in the field is to figure out if there is "life after death." How silly for a Christian to pursue this! For we know that there is life after death, and you either end up in Heaven if you are a follower of God, or you will spend eternity in Hell.

"For God so loved the world that He gave His only begotten Son, that whoever believes in Him should not perish but have everlasting life."

John 3:16 (NKJV)

"Most assuredly, I say to you, he who hears My word and believes in Him who sent Me has everlasting life, and shall not come into judgment, but has passed from death into life."

John 5:24 (NKJV)

Right there, Jesus tells us that there is life after death. The age-old question that so many paranormal investigators pursue is answered! *But wait*, you say, what about the fact that so many ghost hunters and psychics and even lay people who try to communicate with the dead, how come they get pertinent responses from people who have passed over? How is it that a psychic or an EVP will convey a voice or answers that sounds exactly like the person who has died? Isn't that proof that people still hang around on this Earth even after they die? The answer is rather simple. Demonic trickery to get us to think that death is not final. And if death is not final, then there is no need for us to have to believe in God or Heaven or Hell.

Demons have the power to perform minor wonders and signs in order to deceive us. They have superhuman and supernatural ability that goes beyond what we humans can comprehend or understand. Though a discussion for another time, the book of Revelation tells us this: *"It performs great signs, even making fire come down from heaven to Earth in front of people, and by the signs that it is allowed to work in the presence of the beast it deceives those who dwell on Earth..."* (Revelation 13:13-14a ESV). Though this passage speaks of the end times, it still shows us that Satan and his demons have the ability to perform "miracles," signs and wonders that will blow our minds and that we would call supernatural, for even a minor wonder or sign performed by a demon would be beyond anything we humans could ever comprehend or do on our own, making it a great sign and wonder to us of their power as they attempt to deceive us from the truth found in the Bible.

Thus, it is not unreasonable to believe that they can mimic and trick us into believing that we are talking to a deceased friend or loved one, or a deceased person who used to reside in or around whatever location we are investigating. Demons have superhuman knowledge, which makes it perfectly sensible that they are aware of the habits and sayings of our loved ones and friends. It also makes sense that they know their history (they have been around since the beginning) and thus, can pretend to be a "person" who used to frequent, or live in, or built, or had some sort of connection to a location that a paranormal investigator goes to investigate. The Bible teaches us that we only die once. And that death is final. Therefore, it is impossible for us to be able to contact a deceased loved one or friend or for us to be talking to a historic deceased person at a haunted location.

"...*it is appointed for man to die once, and after that comes judgment,*" (Hebrews 9:27 ESV).

Looking into the Biblical foundation behind this further, we find that death is referred to as a place of silence. That means that no "spirits of the dead" will be making noises or talking to us during an investigation.

"*The dead do not praise the Lord, nor any who go down into silence.*" (Psalms 115:17 NKJV).

Let's take a look at how another version translation of that verse to make it clearer: "*It is not the dead who praise the Lord, nor any of those descending into the silence of death.*" (Psalms 115:17 CSB).

Whoa! Let's dig deeper and look at some cross references, shall we?

"*For Sheol cannot thank You, Death cannot praise You; Those who go down to the pit cannot hope for Your truth.*" (Isaiah 38:18 NKJV).

"*For in death there is no remembrance of You; In the grave who will give You thanks?*" (Psalms 6:5 NKJV).

Sheol, to clear up any confusion, is the Hebrew word used to refer to the realm or abode of the dead. It is described as being totally silent, gloomy and devoid of light, with no remembrance and nobody can ever hope to escape it (*"before I go--and I shall not return-- to the land of darkness and deep shadow,"* Job 10:21 ESV).

There is a powerful parable that Jesus tells us that touches on the afterlife. This parable is unique in that Jesus names two of the people in the parable, something that doesn't happen in any other parable. This leads some commentators and scholars to believe that

Jesus is talking about two real people, not just two people He "made up" for the sake of the parable. If this is true that Jesus is talking about what happened to two real people, then this parable contains eye opening truth concerning what happens when we die. Let's take a look:

"There was a rich man who was clothed in purple and fine linen and who feasted sumptuously every day. And at his gate was laid a poor man named Lazarus, covered with sores, who desired to be fed with what fell from the rich man's table. Moreover, even the dogs came and licked his sores. The poor man died and was carried by the angels to Abraham's side. The rich man also died and was buried, and in Hades, being in torment, he lifted up his eyes and saw Abraham far off and Lazarus at his side. And he called out, 'Father Abraham, have mercy on me, and send Lazarus to dip the end of his finger in water and cool my tongue, for I am in anguish in this flame.' But Abraham said, 'Child, remember that you in your lifetime received your good things, and Lazarus in like manner bad things; but now he is comforted here, and you are in anguish. And besides all this, between us and you a great chasm has been fixed, in order that those who would pass from here to you may not be able, and none may cross from there to us.' And he said, 'Then I beg you, father, to send him to my father's house—for I have five brothers— so that he may warn them, lest they also come into this place of torment.' But Abraham said, 'They have Moses and the Prophets; let them hear them.' And he said, 'No, father Abraham, but if someone goes to them from the dead, they will repent.' He said to him, 'If they do not hear Moses and the Prophets, neither will they be convinced if someone should rise from the dead.'"

Luke 16:19-31 (ESV)

This is a powerful passage that has a lot of truth for us to dig into. This parable makes clear that once we die, we will immediately be aware of where we are. We will be consciously aware that we are either in heaven or in hell. There is no middle ground, nor will we be back on Earth in spirit form. This is why the rich man requested merely to be comforted as well as to have a warning sent to his brothers. He was no longer able to interact with the world of the living on Earth.

We see in this passage that the rich man even asks for Lazarus to be sent back to his brothers, who were still alive on Earth, in order for Lazarus to warn them about hell. And his request was denied. *"If they do not hear Moses and the Prophets (that is, if they do not believe what the Bible tells them), neither will they be convinced if someone should rise up from the dead."* (Luke 16:31 ESV) was the response. Wow. In that one sentence, Jesus tells us that we have all the answers we need to understand and know what happens after we die right here in our Bibles. While Jesus was making a reference to His future death and resurrection here, I also believe that verse has even more implication and meaning for today. In today's age, people are very much "need-to-see-it-to-believe-it" and "instant gratification" people. "If someone actually comes back and tells me heaven and hell is real, I'll believe it." But in our age, as I've explored so much in this book, if someone were to appear who had died, we would more likely than not be apt to say, "Oh! I see a ghost! Ghosts are real!" and we would miss the point of what the person came back to say because of what society has taught us about ghosts. We would then set out to tell our amazing ghost story to anyone who would listen and dive into trying to document more proof of that ghosts exist to further support what you encountered. This story shows us that death is it, there is no coming back and interacting with the living once we die.

Death is final. The dead are no longer connected to or in communication with this world. There is no "unfinished business" that they need to take care of. There is no "attached to this place" or "died so suddenly they don't know they are dead" to explain why a "spirit" is still hanging around a location. Demons look to prey on people and places of suffering and great or sudden pain make perfect locations for them to hang around. What better way to deceive people than to make us think that they are the spirits of the deceased still hanging around? We humans are stubborn and born with an innate desire to run away from God. If demons can convince us that death is not final, then there is no need for us to turn to God or read His Word. That, my friends, is a major victory for the Enemy and his demons. Think of it this way: If we are able to "stick around" and hangout as spirits on the Earth after we die, then we have more or less "defeated" death. And that waters down if not entirely negates Jesus's death on the Cross and victory over death and the grave when He rose alive three days later! Not to mention it negates the need for heaven or hell if we can just stick around on Earth. But get this, if we were all just to die and become spirits, why is the world not stuffed with spirits of the dead? Why is George Washington or Michelangelo or Alexander the Great not still hanging around? And an even bigger question is, if we can hang around as spirits after we die, where are all the ghosts of former paranormal investigators? Why are they not hanging around and helping us from the afterlife? Don't you think helping living paranormal investigators learn about the afterlife would qualify as "unfinished business?" See how when we deviate from what the Bible tells us, we end up with so many more questions than answers? If there was a "spiritual in between" or if we actually did "stick around" as spirits after we died, don't you think the Bible would tell us about it? Instead, the Bible tells us that death is final and that the spirits of the dead are unable to talk to the living.

Chapter 4
ELECTRONIC VOICE PHENOMENA

Anyone familiar with ghost hunting or paranormal investigation will have at least heard the term, EVP. EVP stands for Electronic Voice Phenomena and describes voices of spirits being captured and recorded on audio devices that were not heard at the time of recording. This is not to be confused with a disembodied voice, which is a voice that is physically heard by one or more people present, but there is no explanation for where that voice came from.

In the field of paranormal research, EVPs are considered to be the most compelling piece of evidence that we have for proof of the existence of ghosts and spirits. And rightly so. I can tell you firsthand how exciting and mind blowing it is to hear a voice captured on audio that was not heard when I was there in person. It is even more mind boggling when you ask a question or make a statement, and upon review of the audio, you hear a response that is intelligently answering the question you just asked or to a statement you just made. Put any hardcore skeptic in a room with a digital recorder, have them ask a few questions and then ask them to explain any voices that are captured that shouldn't be there. It will leave them scratching their head. Now the spirit world is not an "on command" world where they will perform on cue, but when you get voices in the silence, it will make you wonder about the spirit world and if ghosts are real. Let's dive into these phenomena known as EVP.

One of the biggest theories concerning EVP is that they are the voices of the dead speaking to us. Many times, the responses or communications that get recorded seem to line up with the history of the location or seem to be from someone who used to live in that particular location. Thus, it would appear that ghosts and spirits are real, and that the spirits of some dead people hang around after death. As we read in the *What the Bible Says About Death* section, we can see that it is impossible for the voices captured on EVP to be the voices of a deceased person. What are the voices then? Where do they come from? Simple. They are demons speaking to us. The Bible makes it clear that demons can speak. Take Matthew 8:29 for example: *"And behold, they cried out, saying, 'What do you have to do with us, Son of God? Have you come here to torment us before the time?'"* (Matthew 8:29 LEB). The demons in this passage are clearly talking to Jesus and thus, it would make sense that they can still talk today.

If you've ever watched a ghost hunting show or talked to paranormal investigators, you are probably aware that one of the biggest mysteries surrounding EVP is the fact that oftentimes, only one device will capture the voice whilst all other devices and even people present will not hear it. There is a practical explanation to this as well as some biblical thoughts on why this is true. Imagine you are in a room that is full of people, and you want to say something only to one person. If you are across the room from that person, you're not just going to yell out what you have to tell them for the whole room to hear, you are going to walk over to them and then tell them just loud enough so they can hear you. There might be one or more people standing close by, but they won't hear you because you are not speaking so they can hear you. Same as if you are hanging out with a group of friends, but only want to tell a certain friend something. It is therefore not a stretch to think that a demon can speak just loud enough or specifically for one device to capture. But why just one person? Well, there are three reasons I can think of. Firstly, what better way to keep people focused on investigating the paranormal and keep people scratching their heads than to speak only to one device or person? I mean, you have investigators who have been ghost hunting their whole lives and they are still scratching their heads over how only one device will record an EVP.

Thus, they are focusing their time and effort on the paranormal more than they are on strengthening their walk with God and reading the Bible. Secondly, if a particular person, or persons, on a ghost hunt are more actively involved in the occult and spiritism practices, any demons present will be well aware of that and be focused on those individuals. This ultimately keeps those individuals focused on and enforcing their beliefs and practices in the spirit realm and turned away from God and biblical truths. Thirdly, if Christians are involved in the ghost hunt, demons will try their hardest to corrupt them. We, as Christians, are involved in spiritual warfare every second of every day, and anything demons can use to their advantage is a win for them, and they will use it. If a demon can turn a Christian's focus from God and cause them to start focusing more on ghosts, life after death, and the spirit realm, then that is a huge win for the demon as they are weakening that Christian.

Now, a demon can never cause a Christian to lose their salvation, but by walking farther away from God and focusing on the world and demonic influences, that is going to cause the Christian to inadvertently spread false doctrine and ultimately not be leading people to Christ. This is a huge win for the enemy and demons.

Now I am going to touch on an EVP theory that is a pet peeve of mine. This will be tackled more from a scientific standpoint than biblical, but for any paranormal researchers and ghost hunters out there, and anyone who has ever watched ghost hunting shows, you'll need to hear this.

Theory: *We use digital recorders because spirits speak on frequencies we can't hear. But the digital recorder hears it and plays it back at a frequency we can hear.*

Okay. This is laughable when you put any sort of critical thought to it but sadly, it is a prevalent theory nonetheless, and one I was sadly a proponent of too. Let's dismantle this, shall we? The human ear can hear between 20hz and 20khz, and that is when we are younger, and our ears are in perfect condition. Some people can hear a little lower, some people a little higher, but that is not common. Most people hear a much narrower range of frequencies. As we get older, we lose the ability to hear the higher and lower ends of the frequency chart. I personally can hear about 60hz-16.5khz, and that will narrow the older I get. When you look at voices, the female voice ranges from about 350hz to 17khz, and the male voice from 100hz to 8khz. Both voice spectrums fall well within the range of human hearing. (**source: https://www.seaindia.in/human-voice-frequency-range/)

Now let's look at digital recorders. Most digital recorders consist of four main parts. The interface (buttons, screen, etc.), built in microphone, and most will also have a built-in speaker and hard drive/memory. The microphones are what we are going to focus on here as they are what capture (hear) the sound that gets recorded. Most digital recorders that ghost hunters use consist of voice recorders. These are usually cheaper recorders meant for taking voice notations or recording meetings/lectures. What does this mean? First, being cheaper, they are going to have a low-quality microphone capsule. This means the frequency response is going to be narrow and the sound recorded is not going to be very high quality. Secondly, being a voice recorder, they are designed with voice capture in mind. Thus, many of the cheaper digital recorders are going to have a frequency response more around the 100hz-17khz range, if not narrower. Teams and individuals that are a bit more serious about paranormal investigation will usually invest in a higher quality digital audio recorder. These recorders would include the likes of the Tascam DR-05, Zoom H1 on the cheaper end (if you call $100 cheap) and even up to a Tascam DR-100 Mk3 or Zoom H6 on the pricier end ($300-400). And you can go even more expensive too if you want, even adding higher quality, professional level external microphones. These recorders were designed for high quality audio capture. And being $100+, they are built to capture quality sounding audio. All these recorders have high-quality built-in microphones, and the more expensive ones even have options for recording via professional level external microphones. The built-in mics in these recorders all capture the full frequency range of human hearing, 20hz to 20khz. That means they will capture any sound that gets made that is possible for the human ear to hear.

Let's apply some basic critical thinking here, shall we? If you are using a good quality recorder that captures the 20hz to 20khz range, what does that mean? That means any sound that gets captured by that recorder occurred in the range of human hearing. That's right. It is impossible for the recorder to capture any sound that would not be possible for a human to hear in the first place! No, when you get older and your hearing degrades and say for example, you can only hear 100hz to 15khz, so any sounds the recorder captures in the 20-99hz range or 15,001-20khz range, you are not going to be able to hear anyway. The recorder does not record a sound and magically play back all sounds at frequencies we can hear. It records them and plays them back at the exact frequency it recorded the sound at. It doesn't matter how high quality or expensive the digital recorder, the microphone, speakers, headphones or audio software you use, if the sound was recorded at a frequency you can't hear, you will never be able to hear it. Thus, the theory that spirits speak on frequencies we can't hear but digital recorders can and play them back so we can hear, is impossible.

And whilst we are on the topic of talking to spirits, what about the claims that people claim to hear pets or disembodied animals? Well, the most likely explanation is that demons are imitating an animal to get our attention. This is not too hard to believe. There are many people in the world who can convincingly imitate or mimic different animals and animal sounds. Thus, since demons are supernatural, superhuman creatures, it makes perfect sense that they too can convincingly imitate and mimic animal sounds.

The Bible makes it clear that spiritual entities can talk to humans. Anyone familiar with Christmas knows the story of Jesus's birth and how the angels appeared to Mary and the shepherds and proclaimed the news of the Savior's birth. A further reading of the New Testament reveals Jesus talked directly to demons, and the demons responded back. In the book of Acts, you even read of the Sons of Sceva having a conversation, albeit a short one, that did not end well for them, with demons.

Chapter 5
WHO DO PSYCHICS AND MEDIUMS TALK TO?

We were co-hosting a ghost tour at an old theatre, and I was up in the unrenovated section of the theatre before the event attendees were led up for the tour. I was with the group of event coordinators, one of whom claimed to be a medium. When I would investigate, I always steered clear of psychics and mediums for a few reasons. The main reason, of course, was that the Bible explicitly speaks about psychics/mediums: Leviticus 19:31 NIV, *"Do not turn to mediums or seek out spiritists, for you will be defiled by them. I am the Lord your God."* Let's take a look at how another translation puts this verse, *"Give no regard to mediums and familiar spirits; do not seek after them, to be defiled by them: I am the Lord your God."* (Leviticus 19:31 NKJV). We also didn't believe at the time that their abilities were reliable, consistently reproducible, or even real. This experience would change my perception of their abilities, but not my stance on working or associating with them. We were on the top floor of the building, when the medium and I ended up being the only two people in this room after the others in the group moved to another room.

"I sense a female spirit in here. She is standing by the window, second from the right, waiting for something. Something is keeping her here." the medium said.

"Wait, you sense a spirit of a female in that second window?" I replied.

"Yes. I am not sure if she was killed here or just hanging out, but she is waiting for something."

"Did you talk to the members of the team leading the tour here?" I asked.

"No. I haven't talked to anyone and none of them have talked to me." she replied, turning around to catch up with the rest of the group.

I was stunned. While we were walking over to the building for the performance and investigation, we were walking with the team who was leading the investigation at that building. They had mentioned that there was a spirit of a lady that people would see in the upper room, looking out the second window on the street below. The medium insisted that she had not talked to or been talked to by anyone about this building beforehand and she had never been to that building before either. This experience made me rethink how "fake" all psychics and mediums were. Doing more research, I discovered that while there certainly are many scam psychics and mediums out there, there are a few who are very much legitimate in what they claim that they can do. But exactly who are these psychics talking to and who are they channeling?

Psychics and mediums gain their information through channeling. That is, they are reaching out and contacting a spirit and having that spirit "speak" or convey information to and through the psychic or medium. Channeling can be categorized as divination, which also includes the likes of astrology, horoscopes, tarot cards, palm reading, crystal gazing, seances and other such occult communication practices. These practices are based on the concept that there are spirit beings (spirit guides, familiars, gods, angels, deceased friends or loved ones, etc.) who can communicate with us about the future or about our lives or that hidden information can be divined from certain patterns in nature. Unfortunately, these spirits are all demons and all the patterns in nature are nothing more than coincidences and mankind's attempt to circumvent following and listening to God. As we have seen in the previous sections, any person who dies is no longer able to contact the living. Furthermore, demons use divination as bait to steer a Christian away from God and to entrap a non-Christian into believing that there are benevolent "spirit beings" that can give them guidance *without* having to rely on or believe in God.

Any spirit that responds to a psychic or medium is demonic, and thus the demons aim is to deceive and control the person into following what they say. This is why it is an abomination to God, for we are to seek Him alone for truth and wisdom. Very few people have a true grasp of the deceptive nature and power of spiritism and the dangers that result in partaking in it. While many who "try it out" do not believe it to be real and are just "curious" as they say, they sadly open themselves to the demonic influence, nevertheless. But if one dabbles in spiritism and falls victim to the awe and wonder of it, it is near impossible to break them away from the demonic entanglement they have given themselves over to. Nothing short of earnest prayer and the power of God will be able to bring them out, as Satan and his minions do not lightly let go a prize that they possess.

But just how real is this? How do psychics and mediums seem to be able to give such solid, accurate, credible answers to our questions? If it isn't our loved ones and friends contacting us through the psychic, who is? Many so called "psychics" and "mediums" glean information about a customer through information they can find doing an internet search (friends, family, date of birth, interests, etc.). But what about the ones who know things that should be impossible for them to know? Well, they have gone beyond the stage gimmicks and are dealing with Satan and his demons. *"And no wonder, for Satan himself masquerades as an angel of light. It is not surprising, then, if his servants also masquerade as servants of righteousness. Their end will be what their actions deserve."* (2 Corinthians 11:14-15 NIV). This passage clearly states that Satan and his servants "masquerade as angels of light." What does this mean exactly? It means that Satan and his demons will pretend to be friendly entities that are bearers of truth. Satan deceived Eve and has continued to try to deceive humans ever since. Satan himself is known as "The Deceiver" and the "Father of Lies." Thus, it is no stretch to see that he wants nothing more than to deceive people.

So, then, how does all this work? How do demons give information to psychics and mediums? Well, I have a theory about how this all works. There are too many demons to count, myriads of these buggers all over the world. How do we know this? These Bible passages help us see this, *"But you have come to Mount Zion, to the city of the living God, the heavenly Jerusalem. You have come to thousands upon thousands of angels in joyful assembly,"* (Hebrews 12:22 NIV).

"Then I looked, and I heard the voice of many angels around the throne, the living creatures, and the elders; and the number of them was ten thousand times ten thousand, and thousands of thousands," (Revelation 5:11a NKJV).

Demons are fallen angels. We see this in the following passage where one third of all the angels in heaven rebelled against God alongside Satan.

"Then another sign appeared in heaven: There was a great fiery red dragon having seven heads and ten horns, and on its heads were seven crowns. Its tail swept away a third of the stars in heaven and hurled them to the Earth... Then war broke out in heaven: Michael and his angels fought against the dragon. The dragon and his angels also fought, but he could not prevail, and there was no place for them in heaven any longer. So, the great dragon was thrown out—the ancient serpent, who is called the devil and Satan, the one who deceives the whole world. He was thrown to Earth, and his angels with him."

Revelation 12:3-4a, 7-9 (CSB)

The dragon in this passage is Satan. Angels are sometimes referred to as "stars" and thus this is seen as a reference to the fall of Satan when he and his hosts rebelled against God. Thus, we can safely infer from this passage that 1/3 of the angelic beings sided with Satan and are now what we know as demons. Whilst the war and casting out are to happen in the future, this passage is another clear depiction of the spiritual warfare that rages today and will continue to rage until the return of Jesus.

Well, how many demons are there? The Bible doesn't tell us exactly how many angels or demons there are. Depending on the translation, descriptions that try to express the number of angelic beings include "a multitude", "myriads upon myriads", "multitudes upon multitudes" or "ten thousand times ten thousand." Even though one translation states "ten thousand times ten thousand," that is not an exact number. Instead, that is the author's way of expressing, "Hey guys, look, there are a lot of angelic beings. Like, a lot a lot. Try to imagine, say, ten thousand times ten thousand of them." Thus, they are considered an "innumerable source." And one third of an innumerable source is still a lot, like, a lot a lot.

With so many demons around, this is my theory. When a psychic or medium reaches out to contact a deceased loved one or friend, a demon connects with the psychic or medium and pretends to be the person being reached out to. Though demons are not omniscient— that is, all knowing—the demon can reach out to other demons who had information about that person and therefore can relay information back through the psychic or medium that would make it seem that they had connected with the spirit of the deceased person. Since demons possess superhuman and supernatural abilities, it really isn't that "far out" to believe that they can figure out and communicate information at amazingly fast rates to relay through a psychic or medium. This theory holds true for psychic detectives as well. If a psychic takes on an unsolved case, they reach out to their "familiars" for information concerning the persons involved.

Their "familiars" will oftentimes get back to the psychic with a fairly cryptic or riddle-like response that includes information about the case. To do this, I believe the demon, or demons, who are the psychics "familiars" reach out through the demonic network to any of their counterparts who have information regarding the crime and then pass it along to the psychic detective. Through all of this, the "familiar demons" dig their claws deeper into the psychic or medium and keep them focused on the spirit world and not on God. The psychic or medium becomes so entranced and reliant on their "spirit guides" or "familiars" that instead of turning to God for guidance and advice, they seek the advice of their spirit counterparts who, unknown to the psychic or medium, are demons masquerading as friendly, helpful spirits.

But why are people so quick to seek out psychics, mediums, and other forms of divination? There are many reasons. Some are seeking guidance. Some are unsure of their future and want to know what is in store for them, and while demons are not omniscient (only God is omniscient) and do not know the future, due to their experience and knowledge of the world they can make educated guesses concerning the future. Some people are grieving and struggling with the loss of a friend or loved one and can't let go, thus when it seems like a psychic or medium is able to contact and communicate with the deceased friend or loved one, the person feels some relief. But sadly, it is a false comfort and demonic deception. Some are scared of death. Some are hoping for some advice that gets them rich quick. There is a common joke that says, "If psychics are real, why don't they win the lottery?"

Let's touch on one more thing concerning psychics and mediums and take a look in the Old Testament at Isaiah 8:18-20. This is how the CSB renders the text,

"Here I am with the children the Lord has given me to be signs and wonders in Israel from the Lord of Armies who dwells on Mount Zion. When they say to you, 'Inquire of the mediums and the

spiritists who chirp and mutter,' shouldn't a people inquire of their God? Should they inquire of the dead on behalf of the living? Go to God's instruction and testimony! If they do not speak according to this word, there will be no dawn for them."

This is a really interesting passage of Scripture that answers one big paranormal question for us and also contrasts how mediums provide information with how the Bible provides information. Should people inquire of the dead on behalf of the living? The Bible gives a solid and irrefutable answer. No. We should go to God's instruction and testimony, that is, the Bible. It is also an interesting comparison to see how the Bible describes the way psychics and mediums and how the spirits involved convey their information. It is described as "who chirp and mutter." While this seems to be an odd set of wording, it tells us that the information is not clear, is conveyed quietly and hidden. This is completely opposite of God's instruction and testimony which is clear and distinct.

Sadly, we are seeing a huge increase in spiritism and psychics in recent years. As America gets more secular, people are turning more away from God and seeking a humanistic answer to life's questions. While there is a God who created everything and knows the beginning and the end, people are turning to a dark side of supernatural forces in their search for answers. With tarot cards, psychics, crystals, fortune tellers and more, people are opening themselves up to demonic influence and pushing God out of the equation. And what is sad is that the answers that people are so desperately seeking are all right there in the truth of the Bible. How then does God want us to go about discerning His will for our lives? The answer is a simple one, and powerful. Read your Bible and pray for wisdom. *"If any of you lacks wisdom, let him ask of God, who gives to all liberally and without reproach, and it will be given to him."* (James 1:5 CSB)

Daniel McAdams

Chapter 6
SAUL AND THE
MEDIUM OF ENDOR

After having read the section on psychics and mediums, you might be surprised to find out that the Bible actually includes a story of when someone consulted a medium. In the Old Testament, Israel's first king, King Saul, consults a medium (or witch, depending on which translation that you use) after the prophet Samuel dies. Saul was preparing for a battle with the Philistines, and King Saul wanted to seek advice from the Lord for how to proceed, but the Lord was silent due to Saul having turned away from following the Lord. Earlier in his reign, Saul had banished all mediums from Israel, but in his desperation and fear, he sought out a medium in order to try to contact the spirit of the prophet Samuel in order that he might get a word of good news concerning the upcoming battle. But before you get any notion that this passage of Scripture is supporting the use of mediums and affirming their abilities, let's dive into the passage and see what exactly we find:

"By this time Samuel had died, all Israel had mourned for him and buried him in Ramah, his city, and Saul had removed the mediums and spiritists from the land. The Philistines gathered and camped at Shunem. So, Saul gathered all Israel, and they camped at Gilboa. When Saul saw the Philistine camp, he was afraid and his heart pounded. He inquired of the Lord, but the Lord did not answer him in dreams or by the Urim or by the prophets. Saul then said to his servants, 'Find me a woman who is a medium, so I can go and consult her.' His servants replied, 'There is a woman at En-dor who is a medium.' Saul disguised himself by putting on different clothes and set out with two of his men. They came to the woman at night,

and Saul said, 'Consult a spirit for me. Bring up for me the one I tell you.' But the woman said to him, 'You surely know what Saul has done, how he has cut off the mediums and spiritists from the land. Why are you setting a trap for me to get me killed?' Then Saul swore to her by the Lord, 'As surely as the Lord lives, no punishment will come to you from this.' 'Who is it that you want me to bring up for you?' the woman asked. 'Bring up Samuel for me,' he answered. When the woman saw Samuel, she screamed, and then she asked Saul, 'Why did you deceive me? You are Saul!' But the king said to her, 'Don't be afraid. What do you see?' 'I see a spirit form coming up out of the Earth,' the woman answered. Then Saul asked her, 'What does he look like?' 'An old man is coming up,' she replied. 'He's wearing a robe.' Then Saul knew that it was Samuel, and he knelt low with his face to the ground and paid homage. 'Why have you disturbed me by bringing me up?' Samuel asked Saul. 'I'm in serious trouble,' replied Saul. 'The Philistines are fighting against me and God has turned away from me. He doesn't answer me anymore, either through the prophets or in dreams. So, I've called on you to tell me what I should do.' Samuel answered, 'Since the Lord has turned away from you and has become your enemy, why are you asking me?'"

1 Samuel 28:3-16 (CSB)

Quite the encounter, isn't it? Whilst Samuel has more to say to Saul, his message is not the focus of this section. Rather, we are going to focus on the medium. As you read this passage, you might be tempted to think to yourself that mediums actually have the ability to raise up and communicate with the spirits of dead people. It would make sense since as soon as Saul tells the medium to raise up Samuel, she sees Samuel shortly thereafter. The Bible does not tell us how the medium performed her ritual or how she brought him up from the dead, as that is neither important, nor something we need to know how it was performed, as the Bible explicitly condemns mediumship, but clearly Samuel comes back to communicate. Saul does not see Samuel himself, and nothing in the passage implies that Samuel was physically visible to all who were present (a full-bodied apparition in ghost hunter terminology). Rather, we read that the medium sees Samuel and acts as the mediator for a conversation between Saul and Samuel. This almost clearly seems to affirm that psychics and mediums have a real ability to both bring back spirits of the dead and to communicate with the dead. Or does it? Let's take a closer look at what happens.

Let me start off with this analogy. One day you walk into your kitchen and suddenly see a mouse go running across the floor and disappear behind the refrigerator. You immediately look for someone who is a pest control expert and find a highly recommended person in your town. You give him a call and he comes out that afternoon to help you with your mouse problem. As you both are standing in the kitchen, the mouse suddenly runs across the floor and the pest control guy screams! Would you be shocked and question how he could ever be called an "expert" and have worked in pest control for so long if the simple sight of a mouse causes him to freak out? Now let's apply this line of thinking with the passage of Scripture. *"'Bring up Samuel for me,' he answered. When the woman saw Samuel, she screamed."* Doesn't that seem a little odd? This woman, who had obviously been trained as a medium and worked as a medium for a while, screamed (or "cried out with a loud voice" depending upon translation) when she saw the spirit of Samuel. This was obviously not her first time consulting the dead, as she was known to be a medium, but one would wonder how she stayed a medium or how anyone took her seriously if she would cry out every time she connected with a spirit. This is a vital clue in the text that points to the fact that it was not her own ability, ritual or power that raised up Samuel, nor was it a demon pretending to be Samuel, but rather God intervening and allowing the spirit of Samuel to come back and deliver one last message. This was beyond anything she had ever experienced before and absolutely shocked her. Demonic deception and trickery cannot compare with what God can do. Yet, I sadly admit that many people are more than content to accept the insignificant of the demonic than the almighty grace and power of God.

What clues point to the fact that this was God's doing, by His power, for His purpose and not the medium or a demon? There are a couple other clues to pay attention to outside of the medium's response. If you remember in the previous section, we looked at a passage from Isaiah that refers to mediums and spiritists who communicate through "chirps and mutters" and not through clear statements. Here we see a very clear and understandable message being conveyed from Samuel to Saul through the medium. She wasn't chirping or muttering or conveying a vague message that was hard to make out. Another clue to look for is in the Hebrew itself. The usual Hebrew words (nephesh, tsel) that refer to a person's spirit or soul can also be translated to mean "shade", "shadow", "breath" and "wind." None of those words convey having a solid and detailed figure. Nor is the Hebrew word "yiddeoni" used. "Yiddeoni" can be translated as "familiar spirit" which is what psychics and mediums claim to communicate with. Instead the word translated "spirit" when the medium says, "I see a spirit" is the Hebrew word "elohim." Whilst "elohim" is most commonly used to refer to God, there are also instances of it being used to refer to human beings. This would seem to imply that what the medium was seeing was more substantial than just a normal ghost or spirit-like entity that she was used to (if indeed she had seen or interacted with a visible entity before). She was able to describe details about this figure that made it clear to Saul, beyond a shadow of a doubt, that it was Samuel who she was now communicating with.

Some commentators and scholars see this passage of Scripture as showing that there is legitimacy to what mediums and psychics do. As we explored previously in this book, this is true but only to the extent that it is via demonic trickery. But while we could write hundreds of pages of in-depth study into this passage, the handful of clues I talked about in this book, in my opinion, clearly demonstrates that what happened between Saul, the medium and Samuel was through God's doing and His power for His glory, and not by anything the medium did. Whilst we see that many of the nations around Israel in the Old Testament period relied on mediums and spiritists, that neither confirms nor condones what they do. When we look at this passage in context with the whole of the Bible, it would seem way out of place to include this encounter if this passage is focusing more on what the medium is able to do (thus giving her the glory and power in the story) than on the fact that God is in control of everything, even life and death.

Chapter 7
PHYSICALLY IMPOSSIBLE?

You hear and read these stories all the time. "I saw a ghost and it walked through a wall!" You then think to yourself; *how can something possibly just walk through a wall! That is physically impossible!* Or you'll watch a ghost hunting show or read stories and hear someone ask, "How many spirits are in here?" and a voice will reply with, "30" or "100" or some rather high number. Again, it doesn't seem to make sense. How can there be that many spirits in such a small room? Well, the paranormal community has come up with a theory for both.

To address a spirit walking through walls, paranormal investigators will explain it as being part of a "residual haunting." A residual haunting is supposedly a playback of an event/energy. Such as, a person who used to live in a house made the walk from the living room to the dining room so many times it left an energy imprint. Or the energetic storm of death and destruction at Gettysburg has left a "psychic imprint" on the land and now when conditions are right, you can see the battle or pieces of the battle replay themselves. The reason this theory is used to explain how a ghost just "walks through a wall" is this: the building might have been remodeled since the person died, but to the ghost, they keep walking in the same pattern they were used to in life. So now there might be a wall where once there was a doorway, but to the ghost it is still a doorway, so they keep walking through it. On a quantum physics level, since everything in the universe is made up of atoms and electromagnetic energy, theoretically, if you pushed up against a solid object (say, a wall) for enough time (say, thousands of years), the atoms in your body would eventually meld through the atoms in the wall and you would theoretically be able to walk through the wall.

To address the situation of how there could be 30 or 100 or more spirits in a room, it is less of a theory and more a couple possible explanations. One is that since ghosts and spirits are said to be non-physical, they don't occupy space in the same way we do. Another is that since we don't know exactly what they are, how can we tell what size they are?

Angels are spirit beings. This means they are immaterial and incorporeal. And knowing that demons are fallen angels, this means they are immaterial and incorporeal as well. But though they are spirit beings, they have spatial limitations and temporal limitations as well. Even with these limitations, they can still move swiftly through space. The following verses concerning the angel Gabriel in the Bible show both temporal and spatial limitations for angels (and thus, demons as well). *"While I was still in prayer, Gabriel, the man I had seen in the earlier vision, came to me in swift flight about the time of the evening sacrifice. He instructed me and said to me, 'Daniel, I have now come to give you insight and understanding. As soon as you began to pray, a word went out, which I have come to tell you, for you are highly esteemed. Therefore, consider the word and understand the vision:'"* (Daniel 9:21-23 NIV). Demons, though, are not restricted by physical barriers. The following passage from the Bible gives us insight into the answers to the questions of, "How can a ghost walk through a wall" and "Is it possible for there to be so many spirits in a small space?" Let's take a look:

"Then they came to the other side of the sea, to the country of the Gadarenes. And when He had come out of the boat, immediately there met Him out of the tombs a man with an unclean spirit, who had his dwelling among the tombs; and no one could bind him, not even with chains, because he had often been bound with shackles and chains. And the chains had been pulled apart by him, and the shackles broken in pieces; neither could anyone tame him. And

always, night and day, he was in the mountains and in the tombs, crying out and cutting himself with stones.

When he saw Jesus from afar, he ran and worshiped Him. And he cried out with a loud voice and said, 'What have I to do with You, Jesus, Son of the Most High God? I implore You by God that You do not torment me.'

For He said to him, 'Come out of the man, unclean spirit!' Then He asked him, 'What is your name?'

And he answered, saying, 'My name is Legion; for we are many.' Also, he begged Him earnestly that He would not send them out of the country.

Now a large herd of swine was feeding there near the mountains. So, all the demons begged Him, saying, 'Send us to the swine, that we may enter them.' And at once Jesus gave them permission. Then the unclean spirits went out and entered the swine (there were about two thousand); and the herd ran violently down the steep place into the sea and drowned in the sea."

Mark 5:1-13 (NKJV)

As we see in those verses, a "legion" of demons inhabited one man and then about two thousand pigs. While we do not know the precise number of demons that were involved, we do know that they were many.

But why would a demon spend its days walking through walls? you might ask. That is a good question. Whilst I cannot give you a definitive answer, I can give you a solid possibility. They do this to get your attention. You hear or read about a ghost that is commonly seen "walking through a wall" at a particular location and you are likely going to want to go see it for yourself. Once you go see and believe, you'll start to research ghosts and hauntings and eventually start ghost hunting more. Then you'll start getting communication with the "beyond" and start wondering if there is life after death and how spirits stay around to communicate. Now you are officially focused on the spirit world and trying to figure out life after death with God out of the equation. You are now communing and interacting with demons, having been deceived into thinking that you are just trying to capture evidence of ghosts and figure out how they do what they do. The demon has done its job and has blinded a non-believer to the truth and kept them away from God or caused a believer to become deceived and drawn into the world of the demonic.

Chapter 8
MANIFESTATIONS AND PHYSICAL INTERACTIONS

It was about 5 a.m. in the morning and I had just finished my final rounds for the night in the unit I was in (I was working as a caregiver at this time). I sat down at the kitchen counter and prepared to do my paperwork. When you look out from the kitchen, you look into the dining room. There was an "L" shaped half wall with columns extending to the ceiling that separated the dining room from the hallway to the left and the TV/living room straight ahead. I started to fill out my paperwork when I looked up and my heart stopped. I saw a smokey grey, half-bodied figure walking up the hallway to the left. It was only the upper torso, shoulders and head and didn't have any distinct features, but it was bobbing up and down in clearly a walking motion. I sat frozen as I watched it continue to walk up the hallway, getting closer to the end of the half wall where it would be within a few feet of me. It passed behind one of the columns and disappeared shortly before getting to the end of the half wall. I sat frozen, staring at the area it disappeared...but it never reappeared.

While this wasn't a full-bodied apparition (though I have seen those too), I had seen a human-like figure with my own eyes. It was as real as a person you would walk past on the street or at the grocery store. While full bodied apparitions are considered the "holy grail" of paranormal documentation, people report seeing shadow figures, mists, light anomalies, parts of a human figure (example- an arm reaching through a doorway), but there are times where people report seeing an actual human figure when there should be nobody there. Not only are people seeing things, but there are even physical interactions, either between the person and the entity or the entity and the environment around it. Anything from a door opening or closing on its own, knocking sounds, footsteps, the feeling of being touched, being scratched by an unseen force, and even objects getting thrown across rooms. This is known as a "poltergeist" spirit amongst paranormal investigators and ghost hunters.

This preceding paragraph touches on two big questions in the field of paranormal research. Firstly, how are spirits able to manifest physically? And second, how is a supposedly "unseen," "disembodied," or "non-physical" entity able to interact with the physical environment and even mark people? Well, in my near decade of investigating and research, I have never been able to discover nor have I ever come across any definitive or conclusive answers to these questions. But then I looked in the Bible. Let's take a look at both of these questions.

How can spirits manifest themselves physically to us? I mean, they are supposed to be energetic beings that are non-physical and don't have any bodies. A prevailing theory is that it takes a ton of energy for a spirit to manifest itself physically, and therefore can only appear for a very short period of time. This would make appearing as a mist or fog plausible, as they have no physical "shell" or "container" to keep their energy together, but that doesn't explain why people report seeing shadow figures, parts of human anatomy or even full-bodied figures. This conundrum has therefore led to some more "out there" theories, including theories such as shadow figures and full-bodied apparitions are actually aliens. Or another fairly prominent theory is that there are "creatures" or "entities" that exist on a plane or spectrum we can't see with our own eyes. Well, that second theory is actually spot on and accurate. And when you look in the Bible, you can put a name to the entity/creature: demons and angels.

"While they were perplexed about this, behold, two men stood by them in dazzling apparel. And as they [the disciples] were frightened and bowed their faces to the ground, the men said to them, 'Why do you seek the living among the dead? He is not here but has risen.'"

Luke 24:4-6a (ESV)

"The two angels came to Sodom in the evening, and Lot was sitting in the gate of Sodom. When Lot saw them, he rose to meet them..."

Genesis 19:1a (ESV)

As we see in the first passage, Luke, the author, describes angels as "two men" standing in dazzling clothing. The angels in this passage manifested themselves in the form of men. We also see in that passage that the angels talk to the disciples as well. This goes to show that angels, and by extension, demons, can both manifest and physically appear as humans and talk to humans as well. They have that capability. The second passage from the book of Genesis again describes to angels manifesting physically. The man Lot saw them with his own eyes. Does this ring a bell? Does this not align with many such ghost stories where the witness sees an entity with their own eyes? Demons, being once angels themselves and having the same abilities, can therefore masquerade as "ghosts" or "spirits" and manifest themselves as they so please. Being that they are demons, they are not going to manifest themselves on cue unless they choose to. But they will manifest themselves just often enough to keep people telling stories about what they've seen and keep paranormal investigators and ghost hunters wanting to know more and wanting to keep going out into the field to try to document this "holy grail" of paranormal phenomena for themselves. But being demons, they were once angels, and exist on a spiritual realm that is beyond our own, but fully capable of manifesting in and interacting with our physical reality to keep us believing in "ghosts" and "spirits of the dead" and keep our attention fixated on "spirits of the dead walking the Earth."

If ghosts and spirits are non-corporeal beings, without body or physical form, how is it possible for them to move objects? Or better yet how is it possible for them to scratch or leave a physical mark on a person? One of the theories out there is that they concentrate their "energy" on a particular point or all at once to make an object move. Such as when a concentrated burst of air blows over an empty plastic cup or a gust of wind moves a door. But how can this explain how an entity leaves scratches or marks on a person? To the skeptic and unbeliever, they say this is impossible. But it is something that happens. I have even witnessed it happen personally. During an investigation, one of the investigators I was with suddenly, out of nowhere, developed a large, almost bleeding scratch on the side of his neck as he passed through a doorway. He hadn't been messing with his neck, nobody else had touched him, he never bumped into anything, and less than thirty seconds prior to getting scratched, video clearly showed that his neck was completely clear of any marks. None of us had any explanation for how this happened. But as we saw earlier, demons are able to manifest themselves physically. Does this mean they can physically touch or harm us as well? Let's see what the Bible says,

"Then they brought him a demon-possessed man who was blind and mute, and Jesus healed him, so that he could both talk and see." (Matthew 12:22 NIV).

"As they were going away, behold, a demon-oppressed man who was mute was brought to him. And when the demon had been cast out, the mute man spoke..." (Matthew 9:32-33a ESV).

We see here in these passages that demons caused people to be both blind and also mute. These passages hit close to home for me due to my experience I had which I mentioned in the introduction. Another passage that shows the power that demons can have over a person is found in the Gospel of Mark:

> *"And they brought the boy to Him. And when the spirit saw Him, immediately it convulsed the boy, and he fell on the ground and rolled about, foaming at the mouth. And Jesus asked his father, 'How long has this been happening to him?' And he said, 'From childhood. And it has often cast him into fire and into water, to destroy him. But if you can do anything, have compassion on us and help us.' And Jesus said to him, 'If you can! All things are possible for one who believes.'"*

Mark 9:20-23 (ESV)

If demons are capable of causing these ailments and are able to physically control a person, it is not impossible to believe they could leave scratches or other physical marks as well. We see in nature; intense heat waves can cause injury. Now, this isn't a physical, solid object hitting or interacting with a person, but superheated air. Superheated or supercooled air, while not a solid object, can cause injury to humans. Thus, it is not too great a stretch to believe that demons, with their superhuman and supernatural abilities, can exercise minor control over their immediate environment to cause a physical injury, such as a burn or scratch, to a person. The Bible also records times where angels struck down the enemies of God's people. While this was allowed by God, it shows that angelic beings have that power as well

These passages of Scripture also help us find answers to another question in the paranormal field. That is the question of, "Are people really demon possessed or is it all just a health or medical concern?" Many non-believers in the paranormal and scientists are quick to scoff at the idea that a person could be demon possessed. They laugh it off and call paranormal investigators crazy for even considering that could be a possibility. Even some Christian scientists and medical experts are quick to say that demon possession isn't a thing, but rather the person just has a health or medical issue. But as we see from the above passages of Scripture, we see that demonic possession can be the cause of physical ailments and health conditions. There is another verse that clearly states that there is a difference between being demon possessed and having a health issue.

> *"Then the news about him spread throughout Syria. So, they brought to Him all those who were afflicted, those suffering from various diseases and intense pains, the demon-possessed, the epileptics, and the paralytics. And He healed them."*

Matthew 4:24 (CSB)

Here we see that Jesus not only healed health and medical conditions, but He also healed the demon possessed. Why, pray tell, would Matthew feel the need to tell us that Jesus healed the demon possessed and make it a separate statement, if it was nothing more than a non-demonic health or medical condition? This shows that people can suffer from demonic possession. We see that some of the demons made mention of Christ's divinity when He was confronting them, even when the disciples had failed to realize that. How would epilepsy or another medical condition impart knowledge like that? It can't. But we must not be quick to diagnose people who are acting "demon-possessed" as being demon-possessed too quickly. Not all health and medical conditions are caused by demons, and failure to get someone proper medical help in an effort to "drive out a demon" could lead to some serious and sometimes fatal and legal consequences for those involved.

I am going to quickly touch on another paranormal topic as it relates to manifestation and being able to see spirits. There is a theory that pets, especially cats and dogs, are more sensitive to the spirit world and can see spirits that we can't. There are many stories out there about "my pet would stare down the hallway and then I would hear the door close when nobody else was home" or something along those lines. Many paranormal "experts" are quick to say that because animals have much more sensitive senses than us humans, that they are easily and reliably able to pick up on spiritual and paranormal activity. It isn't uncommon to see a ghost hunting team take a pet dog with them and then wait to see if the dog responds oddly in an area to then validate that there are indeed ghosts there. You'll find many articles on blogs and paranormal websites that go into elaborate detail on how animals are able to perceive the spirit world. But can they really see spirits and ghosts?

I am going to give my two cents on this particular topic. I believe that demons know that animals, particularly our pets, have different senses from ours that are more sensitive. Knowing this, knowing how attached we are to our pets, knowing how inquisitive our human minds are, and having supernatural abilities, I believe that demons will manifest themselves just enough for a pet to notice something being different and get them to react. This in turn gets our attention and lead us to believe our pet is now interacting with "the beyond" or a dead loved one. And if a demon can use our pets to lead us to believe that a "dead loved one" is still with us, or that ghosts and spirits are real, they know we will most likely start looking for answers in the secular realm and turn our attention from being focused on God. But, knowing that our pets have different senses that are more sensitive than ours, it is also entirely possible that your pet is reacting to a bug or small animal being in a hard-to-access part of your house, or to a creaking sound or to natural sounds that lie just outside our ability to hear, or maybe your pet suddenly just got lost in thought or dozed off staring into space for a minute or two. Hey, that happens to me every once in a while. I will conclude this section with a passage from Scripture detailing Job's encounter with a demon:

> " *Now a word was brought to me stealthily;*
> *my ear received the whisper of it.*
> *Amid thoughts from visions of the night*
> *when deep sleep falls on men,*
> *dread came upon me, and trembling,*
> *which made all my bones shake.*
> *A spirit glided past my face;*
> *the hair of my flesh stood up.*

It stood still,
but I could not discern its appearance.
A form was before my eyes;
there was silence, then I heard a voice:"

Job 4:12-16 (ESV)

Chapter 9
MORE ABOUT DEMONS

Ask any paranormal investigator about demons and they will tell you that you have nothing to be afraid of and that demonic hauntings are rare. They'll tell you that the majority of the spirits out there that you'll come into contact with are friendly, benevolent spirits of deceased souls and that while you'll occasionally come across a malevolent or mean spirit, that you will probably never come across a demonic haunting. Watch any of the TV shows or online ghost hunting videos and they'll use "demonic hauntings" to get the ratings and make that particular episode seem more extreme. The paranormal community, while it accepts that demons are real, does not like to think about actually having to interact with them. Sadly, they have been deceived. Every spirit or entity they come in contact with is just that, a demon.

Throughout the sections above, we have clearly identified the source of paranormal activity. This source is demons. This is not what any ghost hunter, paranormal investigator, parapsychologist, or psychic wants to hear. "But we have proof that we are talking to the spirit of a dead person, not a demon!" you'll hear them say, and I've claimed that myself before, too. "99% percent of the spirits we come in contact with are nice and don't have a single harmful bone in their body! Wait…ghosts don't have bones…no harmful side to them!" they'll cry out in their defense. But sadly, this is all caused by demonic deception. Demons disguising themselves as benevolent, friendly spirits and masquerading as the "spirit of a dead person" on Earth. But the more you investigate the Bible and the more you consider demons as the answer to the questions and theories that persist in the world of paranormal investigation, the more answers you'll discover are becoming answered.

Are all demons evil? If all ghosts and spirits are demons, why then do all these paranormal investigators insist that the majority of hauntings are from benevolent, harmless entities? Throughout the New Testament, we are warned about Satan and his demons. Mark 1:27 refers to demons as "unclean spirits." 1 Kings 22:23 refers to demons as "deceiving spirits." Ephesians 6:12 (CSB) states concerning demons, *"For our struggle is not against flesh and blood, but against the rulers, against the authorities, against the cosmic powers of this darkness, against evil, spiritual forces in the heavens."* It is made clear in the Bible that demons are not benevolent, friendly spirits. But they will sure pretend to be to keep people interested and involved in ghost hunting. Why? Because who would want to believe in ghosts and go ghost hunting if all that happened was dark and evil activity? That would be very counterproductive. As 2 Corinthians 11:14b (CSB) tells us, *"And no wonder! For Satan disguises himself as an angel of light."*

But what harm can they really do? As we have seen in the New Testament, Jesus spent much of His time on Earth performing miracles of healing on people who were demon possessed. We see that demons caused a range of physical ailments from going mad to being blind and mute. But beyond physical ailments, demons can cause significant spiritual harm to humans. What can Satan and his demons do?

- Satan and his demons can blind the minds of unbelievers from the Gospel. *"In their case, the god of this age has blinded the minds of the unbelievers to keep them from seeing the light of the gospel of the glory of Christ, who is the image of God."* (2 Corinthians 4:4 CSB).

- Satan and his demons promote false doctrine to deceive both believers and unbelievers. *"Now the Spirit explicitly says that in later times some will depart from the faith, paying attention*

> *to deceitful spirits and the teachings of demons, through the hypocrisy of liars whose consciences are seared."* (1 Timothy 4:1-2 CSB).

- Satan and his demons can perform signs and wonders to deceive us. *"Then I saw three unclean spirits like frogs coming from the dragon's mouth, from the beast's mouth, and from the mouth of the false prophet. For they are demonic spirits performing signs, who travel to the kings of the whole world to assemble them for the battle on the great day of God, the Almighty."* (Revelation 16:13-14 CSB).

And while that passage is speaking about the future and the end times, with what we have explored in this book, it is clear that demons can perform signs and wonders today to deceive us and they will continue to do so up until Satan and his demons are defeated and thrown into the lake of fire in the end times.

How, then can you stand up to and defend yourself from demons? The answer is by turning to Jesus, putting your faith in Him and accepting Him as your Lord and Savior. By spending time in the Bible and in communion with God, you are building up your defenses against Satan and his demonic attacks. *"Therefore, submit to God. Resist the devil, and he will flee from you."* (James 4:7 CSB). A very encouraging statement is made in the book of Colossians concerning our spiritual warfare. *"He disarmed the rulers and authorities and disgraced them publicly; He triumphed over them in Him."* (Colossians 2:15 CSB). Through His death on the cross, Jesus triumphed over Satan and his demons, and now through Him, we too share in that victory.

As a Christian, put on the full armor of God and you will be equipping yourself to stand firm against Satan and his demons in their attempt to sway you from your walk with God.

"Finally, be strengthened by the Lord and by his vast strength. Put on the full armor of God so that you can stand against the schemes of the devil. For our struggle is not against flesh and blood, but against the rulers, against the authorities, against the cosmic powers of this darkness, against evil, spiritual forces in the heavens."

Ephesians 6:10-12 (CSB)

We fight against spiritual forces in the heavens. Satan and his demons are real. The spirit world is real. Sadly, so many have already been deceived and believe that demons don't exist or that they can "work with" and/or "control" demons. Demons have tricked many into believing that the dead still roam the Earth and that we can communicate with them. They have even blinded many Christians with this false doctrine as well.

How then, do some Christians and non-Christians alike become so involved in ghost hunting and the paranormal? One way demons gain influence over a person is through that person actively seeking involvement. Some Christians foolishly believe that since they abide in Christ, that they can actively go out and "control" demons. They try to use "the power of Christ" to compel demons to submit to them or to exorcise the demon from a place. Nowhere in Scripture do we find support for us as Christians to actively seek out and confront demons. Rather, we are to confront the forces of darkness by sharing the Gospel and living godly lives. And sadly, once a Christian starts to actively seek out the demonic, they will slowly start to head down a path that leads away from the Bible and become a pawn of Satan, whether they intend to or not. Many non-Christians get involved with the demonic through the belief that they could cast a certain spell or bind the demon using the demon's name. Sadly, this is not the case and in an ironic twist, the person attempting to control the demon becomes themselves controlled and influenced by the demon. Others may not believe that demons are real but are curious about having their own paranormal experiences or seeing whether a Ouija board or other form of divination actually works. And once they get a taste of it, they get sucked in before they ever realize what happened.

Probably the most common cause of demonic influence is sin. Sin is active spiritual rebellion against God. If we know what He wants and what His will is, yet we refuse to submit to Him, we are siding with the spiritual forces who also are actively opposing God, Satan, and his demons. By choosing to ignore God and live a life of sin or pursue a sinful activity, we are making a clear statement that we are opposing God and thus open ourselves up to more demonic influence.

I conclude this section with a heavy word of warning. Demons are no joke and not to be trifled with. No matter how smart you think you are, how strong you think you are or how brave you think you are, demons are more so. They are supernatural beings that have been around long before you were born. When the Bible says to stay away from occult activities and that they are detestable to God, it is not because God is trying to be a killjoy. Rather, He is trying to protect you and keep your focus on Him. Trying to have some "innocent fun" by going on a ghost hunt or playing with a divination tool is no excuse. These activities, as harmless and fun as they may sound, have a direct link to the dark forces that exist in our world. The adrenaline rush might seem cool at the time, and the stories you tell of your experiences might seem cool to tell others, but it is not worth it.

I got involved in the paranormal thinking I was innocently trying to find scientific answers to what was happening. I had no intentions to let my involvement lead me away from God. But the more I got involved, the less time I was spending focusing on God and in the Bible. Inadvertently, I ended up getting heavily involved in New Age spirituality and believing things that were contradictory to the Bible. Towards the end of my paranormal investigation career, I noticed myself becoming more and more intrigued by and interested demons. I would tell people I wasn't afraid of demons because I knew how to handle the situation. Sadly, I was blind to the fact that it was actually the demons who had a handle on me and were influencing me to lead others into the paranormal and therefore, away from God.

Chapter 10
CONCLUSION

For years I had deceived myself into believing a lie. I was a Christian and believed in heaven and hell but still thought that the spirits of the dead roamed the Earth. I even thought that the Bible backed up my claim. I mean, Jesus's disciples saw Him walking on water and thought He was a ghost! In Jesus's time, it was a common held belief that if a person were to die on the sea, that their "ghost" or "spirit" would hover over the water at the site of their death. After His death and resurrection, He appeared to them in a locked room and they were frightened and thought they were seeing a ghost.

Again, there was a widespread belief amongst the Gentiles and some of the Jews in Jesus's time that ghosts existed, even though that ironically contradicted the Jewish belief and teachings concerning the afterlife. And it is not recorded that He rebuked them for believing that ghosts were real, nor was it recorded that Jesus ever said they weren't real. *That right there was my golden ticket*, I thought, to back up what I was doing with the Bible. I also thought that I was going about paranormal investigation in a way that wasn't condemned by the Bible. I thought I was just going out to try to document proof that a location was indeed haunted and to try to gather data and documentation to help study and figure out what these entities were and how they operated. I wasn't trying to uncover hidden information through divination. I wasn't trying to gain supernatural gifts or powers or be like God. I wasn't involved with or trying to become a medium or psychic. And I wasn't using horoscopes or astrology or any other ways and methods that were strictly forbidden by the Bible. But I was not getting anywhere with what I was doing. Whenever I would "kind of" get an answer to a question or theory, many more questions would pop up.

I often found myself answering other people's inquiries and questions with vague, speculative answers, stating that we didn't know the answer yet, but that is why we were in the field, we were trying to find out the answer. But by finally looking at what the Bible says about the spirit world, I see that I was absolutely deceived. When you consider what the Bible says and view paranormal questions and theories with the viewpoint of demons as the answer, so many questions and theories that are out there are answered.

Looking back on what has transpired in the year 2019, I am shocked at the spiritual warfare battle that took place in my life:

- In January, I returned to my old home church and was introduced to expository preaching and a pastor who became a good friend of mine. Immediately after that, my team and I captured the most jaw dropping piece of visual evidence we have ever captured in our lives and I had one of the most personal paranormal encounters of my life too.

- In February, I started spending more time in the Bible. At the same time, my passion to go on ghost hunts was burning stronger than ever too.

- In April, I signed up for and started the Certificate in Biblical Studies program at Online Bible College. Shortly thereafter, we finally gained free access to investigate a location we had been wanting to get into for a while.

- In the spring, I was talking with my boss when the thought, "And there is a possibility that they are all actually demons." randomly pops into my mind and I started considering it. Shortly after that, on an investigation of a location we had been to many times, I had a very creepy but mind-blowing encounter with an unseen entity.

- In June, the pastor at my church preaches an expository sermon from the book of Revelation that makes my jaw drop concerning spiritual warfare and demons. About that same time, my team and I got asked to present at a paranormal conference later in the year, and we didn't even have to submit an inquiry or fill out the official presenter form!

- Over the summer, I worked two, weeklong rodeos for my job and made some good, Christian friends, had great theological talks, and spent much time in Scripture. Just after returning home, I got confirmation that we were reserved to investigate a huge and well-known location in the fall.

- In August, I had an amazing lunch meeting with my pastor and thought-provoking talk on the paranormal. Dillon and I also began to discuss the idea that demons are behind everything in the world of paranormal investigation. Later in August, during the paranormal conference, we were asked to lead all the public investigations planned for the conference weekend and were the only paranormal team present. We had an amazing presentation and constantly had people coming up to us with questions and wanting to know more. Then, we had a paranormal experience that we couldn't begin to comprehend and couldn't believe, an experience at a magnitude that we have never heard or read about, ever.

- In September, I started writing this paper and taking a serious, biblical look at the paranormal world and Dillon and I decided to officially retire from and leave the world of paranormal investigation and pursue our walks with God. We then got contacted by a very prominent and widely read newspaper about them wanting us to take them on a ghost hunt so they can write an article on it for October.

I am shocked by this battle that went on in my life. The more I would turn to God, the more would happen in the paranormal world to try to keep my attention there. The deeper and more incredible experiences I would have in my walk with God and my faith, the greater the magnitude of incredibility we would experience with the paranormal. Satan and his demons were fighting hard to inflate my pride and ego, to keep my attention focused on the paranormal and to keep me blinded to the truth. Well, I am going to close with this. Those of you who have talked with me about the paranormal or who have heard me speak at conventions about the paranormal, you will know that one of my driving mottos in paranormal investigation was:

"I am married to finding the truth. I am not married to the idea of proving whether ghosts and the paranormal are real. I am not married to the idea of proving that they don't exist. I am married to the pursuit of finding the truth."

Well, my friends, I have found the truth. And this is it.

God bless!
Soli Deo gloria
Daniel McAdams

ABOUT THE AUTHOR

Daniel is a former paranormal investigator turned theology student. He holds a Diploma in Radio and Television Broadcasting from Colorado Media School and a Diploma in Biblical Studies from Online Bible College. He is currently pursuing his Associate of Biblical Studies at Andersonville Theological Seminary. Because of his experience in paranormal investigation, Daniel feels uniquely called by God to minister and reach out to those who are currently involved in that pursuit, as well as to those who have been affected by paranormal experiences. His focus is on God and he desires to help anyone, and everyone, turn their focus to God and find victory in Jesus. He lives in Jefferson City, MO and is a member of Concord Baptist Church. He is married to his wonderful wife, Kayli, and has two amazing daughters.